afternoon tea

afternoon tea

British food for lazy days

This edition published in 2011
LOVE FOOD is an imprint of Parragon Books Ltd

Parragon
Queen Street House
4 Queen Street
Bath BA1 1HE, UK

ISBN: 978-1-4454-3793-4

Printed in China

Introduction by Linda Doeser

Notes for the Reader
This book uses both metric and imperial measurements. Follow the same units of measurement throughout; do not mix metric and imperial. All spoon measurements are level: teaspoons are assumed to be 5 ml, and tablespoons are assumed to be 15 ml. Unless otherwise stated, milk is assumed to be full fat, eggs and individual vegetables are medium, and pepper is freshly ground black pepper.

The times given are an approximate guide only. Preparation times differ according to the techniques used by different people and the cooking times may also vary from those given. Optional ingredients, variations or serving suggestions have not been included in the calculations.

Recipes using raw or very lightly cooked eggs should be avoided by infants, the elderly, pregnant women, convalescents and anyone suffering from an illness. Pregnant and breastfeeding women are advised to avoid eating peanuts and peanut products. Sufferers from nut allergies should be aware that some of the ready-made ingredients used in the recipes in this book may contain nuts. Always check the packaging before use.

Contents

Afternoon Tea

Teatime is a quintessentially British ritual that perfectly mirrors the story of Britain's quirky class system. Afternoon tea – served between four and five o'clock – had nothing to do with hunger and everything to do with status and leisure. After a busy morning writing invitations and an exhausting afternoon choosing a new hat, the lady of the house would return to her drawing room, where she and her visitors could relax with delicate sandwiches cut into fingers or triangles, thin slices of bread and butter and an array of tempting cakes and rich pastries. As they sipped their Earl Grey tea, poured into fragile porcelain cups from a silver teapot, they could eye each other's hats – only house guests would not wear one – and gossip happily. Gentlemen would sometimes be present and the younger ones would make themselves useful handing around cups, lifting the silver kettle from its stand and surreptitiously flirting with the older daughters of the house. The children would have their own nursery tea elsewhere. Given that the day had already included both breakfast and luncheon, and a dinner of at least four courses was to follow, and that it was considered courteous for visitors to leave quite promptly, most of this lavish spread was often left untouched.

Tea for manual workers and agricultural labourers was quite a different kind of repast. They would sit at the table between five and six o'clock, together with their children, and enjoy high tea, having eaten their dinner at midday. The menu usually included a filling hot dish in the winter, such as herrings in oatmeal, and cold meat and salad in summer, consumed with plenty of bread and butter – but not in wafer-thin slices – followed by home-made cake. All this would be 'washed down' with numerous cups of strong Indian tea.

Tea for the 'middle' classes, as might be expected, was something of a mix of the two. Having eaten lunch, not luncheon, at one o'clock, they would have high tea on weekdays, often featuring a variety of teacakes, fancy cakes and scones, but aspired to afternoon tea at weekends, especially Sundays. This required the best china and may even account for the rapid growth in the electroplating industry, as ambitious and sometimes snobbish hostesses regarded a china teapot as 'not the done thing'.

The decline of teatime

Like all customs, teatime changed over the years but it hung on in some form or another for much longer than might have been expected. Many formerly wealthy households experienced a drastic decline in income in the years following World War I, with a consequential dwindling of the number of servants and a reduction in their extravagant lifestyle. Young wives who had grown up in the 1920s wanted to run their homes in new ways

and abandoned the stuffy customs of their mothers. Cocktail hour became the society hostess's favourite time. In contrast, the middle classes developed the tea dance. Grand hotels served formal afternoon tea while an orchestra played foxtrots and quicksteps for light-footed patrons.

World War II not only put an end to domestic service, except for the very rich, but also saw a massive growth in the female workforce. A cup of tea and a bun at a teashop was the nearest 'office girls' came to afternoon tea, but many families still ate high tea even as late as the 1960s.

The 'swinging sixties' brought huge changes to British society, including the availability of cheap foreign travel that introduced the insular British to other cuisines, none of which included teatime but most of which featured a glass of wine with dinner. Young people no longer lived in the family home until they got married but led independent lives in flatshares with far too much going on in their exciting young world to stop for tea.

School cookery lessons, which had always featured those perennial favourites, rock cakes and Victoria sponge, were discontinued and takeaway pizzas and supermarket ready meals gradually superseded home cooking in many families.

Completing the circle

In the twenty-first century, with the fashion for grazing rather than family meals, televisions, computers and games consoles in every room and a population that is always running to catch up with itself, it looked as if afternoon tea had become as archaic as the crinoline. Yet it has enjoyed a tremendous revival. Few, if any, still live the life of *Gosford Park*, but nostalgia for a more gracious and leisured way of life has grown. Fashionable 'ladies who lunch' have switched their allegiance to meeting for tea at exclusive hotels. The tea dance was tentatively revived and has proved immensely popular, not just with those who can remember it but with a younger generation too. The community-minded, who may not be able to afford to throw a grand fundraising dinner, throw open their homes for afternoon tea to raise money for their pet charities. On a more direct level, people who nowadays often live far away from their own families have joined groups that take turns to invite the elderly and isolated to tea. Where once it was considered modern to rip out fireplaces and board up chimneys, it is now the vogue to open them up again – and what could be nicer on a chilly Sunday afternoon than to snuggle cosily in front of a log fire with toast and pâté, scones and jam and a plate of chocolate éclairs, even if the tea you're drinking is made with a tea bag in a mug rather than leaves in a silver pot?

Savouries & Sandwiches

Fancy Sandwiches

Makes 24 of each

prawn pinwheels

- 40 g/1½ oz full-fat soft cheese
- 115 g/4 oz canned prawns
- 1 stick celery, very finely chopped
- 1 tbsp mayonnaise
- lemon juice, to taste
- 6 slices bread
- unsalted butter, softened
- salt and white pepper

devilled egg triangles

- 4 hard-boiled large eggs, shelled and finely chopped
- 2 tbsp mayonnaise
- 1 tsp Dijon mustard
- pinch cayenne pepper
- salt and pepper
- 12 slices wholemeal bread
- unsalted butter, softened
- 2 punnets cress

tuna salad round sandwiches

- 200 g/7 oz canned tuna in olive oil, drained
- 3 tbsp mayonnaise
- finely grated rind of 1 lemon
- salt and pepper
- unsalted butter, softened
- 24 thin slices Granary bread
- small bunch fresh parsley, very finely chopped

1 To make the prawn pinwheel filling, put the cheese in a bowl and beat until smooth. Drain, rinse and finely chop the prawns, stir into the cream cheese with the celery and mayonnaise. Add lemon juice and salt and pepper to taste. Trim the crusts off the bread and cut each slice into rectangles about 7.5 x 13 cm/3 x 5½ inch. Flatten each slice with a rolling pin. Use your fingers to press two slices together at the short ends, squeezing to seal the join; repeat to make three more long slices. Very lightly spread the slices with butter, then top with the prawn mixture, taking it to the edges. Working with one long slice at a time, tightly roll up the bread, starting at a short end; repeat with the remaining three long slices. Wrap each slice very tightly in cling film and chill for at least 1 hour. When ready to serve, remove from the fridge and use a serrated knife to thinly slice off both ends to neaten, then cut eight slices from each roll.

2 To make the devilled egg filling, put the eggs in a bowl, add the mayonnaise, mustard and cayenne pepper and stir together. Add salt and pepper to taste. Spread the butter over the bread and spread the devilled egg mixture over six of the slices, then snip cress over the tops. Top with the remaining bread slices, buttered sides down. Use a serrated knife to cut off the crusts, then cut each sandwich into four triangles. Wrap tightly in cling film and chill until ready to serve.

3 To make the tuna salad, flake the tuna into a bowl and beat in the mayonnaise until well blended. Stir in the lemon rind and salt and pepper to taste. Spread the butter over the bread. Use a 5-cm/2-inch round cutter to cut two circles from each slice. Spread the tuna mixture over 24 of the circles, then top with the remaining 24 circles, buttered sides down. Use a knife to neaten the edges, then spread very lightly with butter. Roll the buttered edges in the parsley. Stack the sandwiches, then wrap very tightly in cling film and chill until ready to serve.

Cheese & Sun-dried Tomato Toasts

Serves 4

- 2 small baguettes
- 175 ml/6 fl oz sun-dried tomato paste
- 300 g/10½ oz buffalo mozzarella cheese, drained and diced
- 1½ tsp dried oregano
- pepper
- 2–3 tbsp olive oil

1 Preheat the grill to a medium–high setting and preheat the oven to 220°C/425°F/Gas Mark 7. Slice the loaves diagonally and discard the end pieces. Place the slices of bread on the rack in the grill pan and toast on both sides until golden.

2 Spread one side of each toast with the sun-dried tomato paste and top with mozzarella. Sprinkle with oregano and season to taste with pepper.

3 Put the toasts on a large baking sheet and drizzle with oil. Bake in the preheated oven for 5 minutes, or until the cheese is melted and bubbling. Remove the toasts from the oven and leave to stand for 5 minutes before serving.

Crab Cake Toasts

Serves 4

- 3 slices white bread, crusts removed
- 2 tbsp milk
- 55 g/2 oz butter, melted
- 175 g/6 oz canned crabmeat, drained, or 150 g/5½ oz fresh or frozen crabmeat, thawed if frozen
- 1 green chilli, deseeded and chopped
- 1 spring onion, finely chopped
- salt and pepper
- lemon wedges, to serve

1 Place one piece of bread on a plate and spoon the milk evenly over it. Leave to stand for a few minutes. Brush the remaining slices lightly on both sides with butter.

2 Mix the crabmeat, chilli and spring onion in a bowl. Mash the soggy bread with a fork and mix it with the crabmeat, scraping in the milk off the plate. Stir in the remaining melted butter and season to taste.

3 Preheat the grill to medium–high and toast the buttered bread on the rack in the grill pan, until crisp and golden on both sides. Top with the crab mixture, spreading it evenly right over the edges and forking the surface slightly so that it is not too smooth.

4 Place under the grill for about 3 minutes, until the topping is browned. Cut into quarters and serve immediately with lemon wedges for squeezing over the topping.

Smoked Salmon Blinis

Makes 24

- 85 g/3 oz crème fraîche
- finely grated rind of 2 lemons
- 3 tbsp very finely snipped fresh chives, plus extra to garnish
- pepper
- 55 g/2 oz smoked salmon, very finely sliced

blinis

- 85 g/3 oz plain flour
- 1 tsp easy-blend dry yeast
- ½ tsp sugar
- 150 ml/5 fl oz warm water
- 85 g/3 oz buckwheat flour
- 125 ml/4 fl oz warm milk
- 40 g/1½ oz butter, melted and cooled
- 1 large egg, separated
- salt and pepper
- vegetable oil for cooking

1. To make the blinis, stir together the plain flour, yeast and sugar in a bowl. Make a well in the centre and slowly add the water, drawing in the flour from the side to make a wet, lumpy batter. Beat until the batter is smooth, then stir in the buckwheat flour, cover the bowl tightly with a tea towel and set aside for 1 hour, until the batter has risen and the surface is covered with air bubbles.

2. Meanwhile, to make the topping, mix the crème fraîche with the lemon rind, the chives and pepper to taste. Cover and chill until required.

3. Stir together the milk, butter, egg yolk and a generous pinch of salt and pepper, then add to the batter, stirring well until blended. Beat the egg white in a separate bowl until peaks form, and then fold into the batter.

4. Heat a large frying pan over medium heat until you can feel the heat rising, then lightly brush the surface all over with vegetable oil using crumpled kitchen paper. Fill a tablespoon measure two-thirds full with the batter, then drop the batter on to the hot surface so it forms a circle about 5 cm/2 inches across; add as many more as will fit in the pan without touching. Cook for just over a minute, or until the top surface is covered with air holes and the bottom is golden brown and set. Use a palette knife to flip over the blinis and cook until set and golden brown. Transfer to a heatproof plate and keep warm while you cook the remaining batter.

5. To serve, arrange the warm, not hot, blinis on a platter and top each with about 2 teaspoons of the chilled crème fraîche. Lay the salmon strips over the crème fraiche, garnish with chives and serve.

Smoked Fish Pâté

Serves 8

- 900 g/2 lb undyed kipper fillets
- 2 garlic cloves, finely chopped
- 175 ml/6 fl oz olive oil
- 6 tbsp single cream
- salt and pepper
- lemon wedges, to garnish
- oatcakes, to serve

1 Put the kippers in a fish kettle or large frying pan and add cold water to just cover. Bring to the boil, then immediately reduce the heat and poach gently for 10 minutes until tender. If using a frying pan, you may need to do this in batches.

2 Transfer the fish to a chopping board using a fish slice. Remove and discard the skin. Roughly flake the flesh with a fork and remove and discard any remaining tiny bones. Transfer the fish to a saucepan over a low heat, add the garlic and break up the fish with a wooden spoon.

3 Gradually add the oil, beating well after each addition. Add the cream and beat until smooth, but do not allow the mixture to boil.

4 Remove the saucepan from the heat and season to taste with salt, if necessary, and pepper. Spoon the pâté into a serving dish, cover and set aside to cool completely. Chill in the refrigerator until required, for up to 3 days.

5 Serve with lemon wedges and oatcakes.

Cheese & Mustard Scones

Makes 8

- 225 g/8 oz self-raising flour, plus extra for dusting
- 1 tsp baking powder
- pinch of salt
- 50 g/1¾ butter, diced, plus extra for greasing
- 125 g/4½ oz mature Cheddar cheese, grated
- 1 tsp mustard powder
- 150 ml/5 fl oz milk, plus extra for brushing
- pepper

1 Preheat the oven to 220°C/425°F/Gas Mark 7. Lightly grease a baking tray.

2 Sift the flour, baking powder and salt into a mixing bowl. Rub in the butter with your fingertips until the mixture resembles breadcrumbs.

3 Stir in the cheese, mustard and enough milk to form a soft dough.

4 On a lightly floured surface, knead the dough very lightly, then flatten it out with the palm of your hand to a depth of about 2.5 cm/1 inch.

5 Cut the dough into eight wedges with a knife. Brush each one with a little milk and sprinkle with pepper to taste.

6 Bake in a the preheated oven for 10–15 minutes, until golden brown. Transfer the scones to a wire rack and leave to cool slightly before serving.

Stilton & Walnut Tartlets

Makes 6

walnut pastry

- 225 g/8 oz plain flour, plus extra for dusting
- pinch of celery salt
- 100 g/3½ oz cold butter, diced, plus extra for greasing
- 25 g/1 oz walnut halves, chopped
- ice-cold water

filling

- 25 g/1 oz butter
- 2 celery sticks, finely chopped
- 1 small leek, finely chopped
- 200 ml/7 fl oz double cream, plus 2 tbsp
- 200 g/7 oz Stilton cheese
- 3 egg yolks
- salt and pepper

1 Lightly grease a 12-hole muffin tin. Sift the flour with the celery salt into a food processor, add the butter and process until the mixture resembles breadcrumbs. Tip into a large bowl and add the walnuts and a little cold water, just enough to bring the dough together. Turn out on to a lightly floured work surface and cut the dough in half.

2 Roll out the first piece and cut out six 9-cm/3½-inch rounds. Roll out each round to a diameter of 12 cm/4½ inches and use to line the muffin tin. Repeat with the remaining dough. Line each hole with baking paper and fill with baking beans.

3 Preheat the oven to 200°C/400°F/Gas Mark 6. Bake the tartlet cases for 10 minutes. Remove from the oven, then take out the paper and beans.

4 To make the filling, melt the butter in a frying pan over a medium–low heat, add the celery and leek and cook, stirring occasionally, for 15 minutes, until very soft. Add the 2 tablespoons of cream, crumble in the cheese and mix well. Season to taste with salt and pepper. Put the remaining cream in a saucepan and bring to simmering point. Pour on to the egg yolks in a heatproof bowl, stirring constantly.

5 Mix in the cheese mixture and spoon into the tartlet cases. Bake for 10 minutes, then turn the tin around in the oven and bake for a further 5 minutes. Leave the tartlets to cool in the tin for 5 minutes and serve.

Leek & Onion Tartlets

Makes 6

pastry

- butter, for greasing
- 225 g/8 oz ready-made shortcrust pastry
- plain flour, for dusting

filling

- 25 g/1 oz unsalted butter
- 1 onion, thinly sliced
- 450 g/1 lb leeks, thinly sliced
- 2 tsp chopped fresh thyme
- 55 g/2 oz Gruyère cheese, grated
- 3 eggs
- 300 ml/10 fl oz double cream
- salt and pepper

1 Lightly grease six 10-cm/4-inch tartlet tins with butter. Roll out the dough on a lightly floured work surface and stamp out 6 rounds with a 13-cm/5-inch cutter. Ease the dough into the tins, prick the bases and leave to chill for 30 minutes.

2 Preheat the oven to 190ºC/375ºF/Gas Mark 5. Line the pastry cases with foil and baking beans, then place on a baking sheet and bake for 8 minutes. Remove the foil and beans and bake for a further 2 minutes. Transfer the tins to a wire rack to cool. Reduce the oven temperature to 180ºC/350ºF/Gas Mark 4.

3 Meanwhile, make the filling. Melt the butter in a large, heavy-based frying pan. Add the onion and cook, stirring constantly, for 5 minutes, or until softened. Add the leeks and thyme and cook, stirring, for 10 minutes, or until softened. Divide the leek mixture between the tartlet cases. Sprinkle with Gruyère cheese.

4 Lightly beat the eggs with the cream and season to taste with salt and pepper. Place the tartlet tins on a baking sheet and divide the egg mixture between them. Bake in the preheated oven for 15 minutes, or until the filling is set and golden brown. Transfer to a wire rack to cool slightly before removing from the tins and serving.

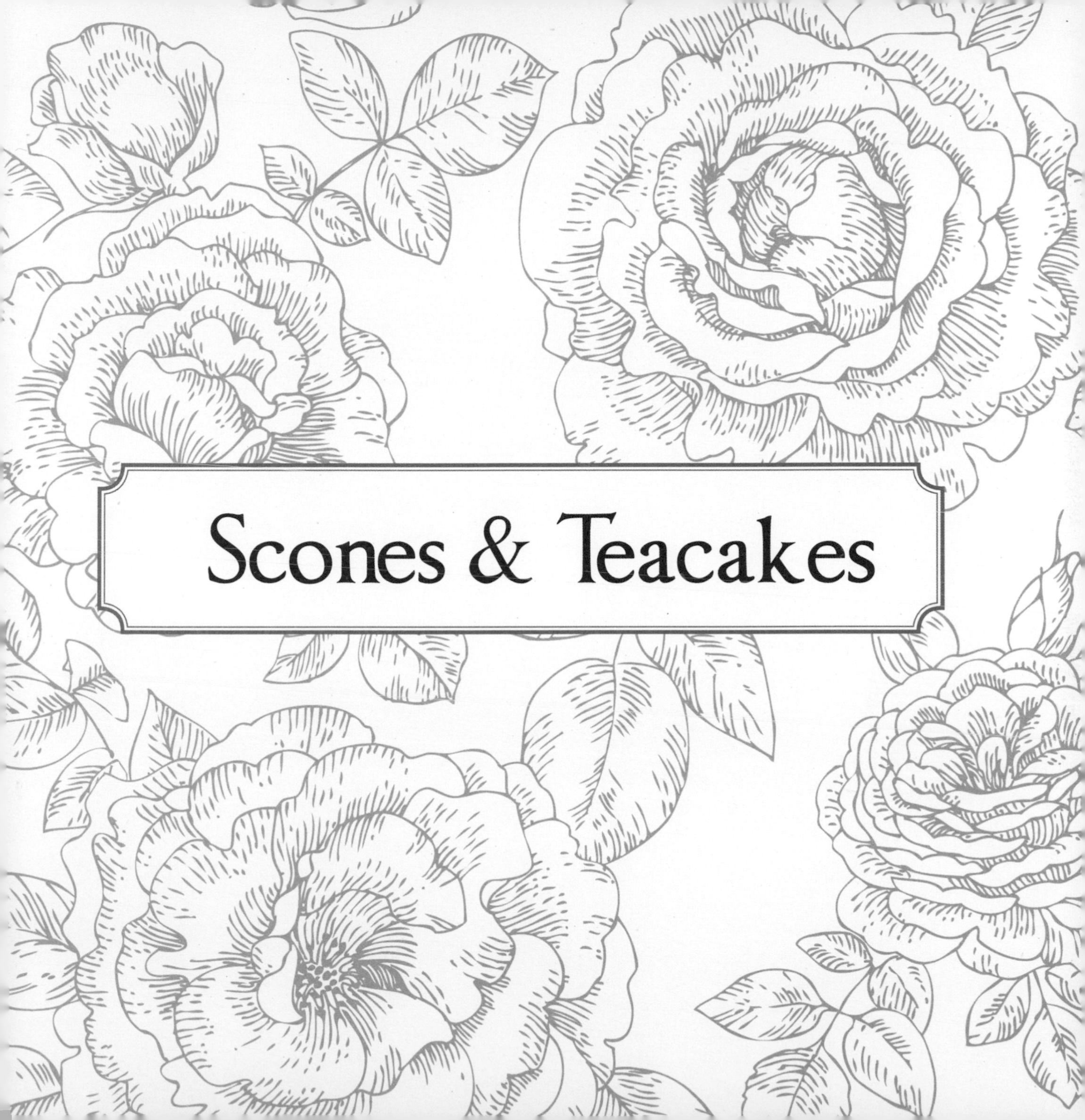

Scones & Teacakes

Traditional Scones

Makes 10

- 450 g/1 lb plain flour, plus extra for dusting
- ½ tsp salt
- 2 tsp baking powder
- 55 g/2 oz butter
- 2 tbsp caster sugar
- 250 ml/9 fl oz milk
- 3 tbsp milk, for glazing
- strawberry jam (page 40) and clotted cream, to serve

1 Preheat the oven to 220°C/425°F/Gas Mark 7. Sift the flour, salt and baking powder into a bowl. Rub in the butter until the mixture resembles breadcrumbs. Stir in the sugar. Make a well in the centre and pour in the milk. Stir in using a palette knife and make a soft dough.

2 Turn the mixture onto a floured surface and lightly flatten the dough until it is of an even thickness, about 1 cm/½ inch. Don't be heavy-handed, scones need a light touch. Use a 6-cm/2½-inch pastry cutter to cut out the scones and place on the baking tray. Glaze with a little milk and bake for 10–12 minutes, until golden and well risen.

3 Remove from the oven and cool on a wire rack. Serve freshly baked with strawberry jam and clotted cream.

Orange & Banana Scones

Makes 12

- sunflower oil, for oiling
- 150 g/5½ oz white self-raising flour, plus extra for dusting, and for rolling, if needed
- 150 g/5½ oz light brown self-raising flour
- 1 tsp baking powder
- ½ tsp ground cinnamon
- 75 g/2¾ oz unsalted butter, diced and chilled
- 50 g/1¾ oz demerara sugar
- 150 ml/5 fl oz milk, plus extra for brushing
- 1 ripe banana, peeled and mashed
- finely grated rind of 1 orange
- 150 g/5½ oz fresh raspberries, lightly mashed

1 Preheat the oven to 200°C/400°F/Gas Mark 6. Lightly oil a baking sheet.

2 Mix the flours, baking powder and cinnamon together in a large bowl, add the butter and rub in with your fingertips until the mixture resembles breadcrumbs. Stir in the sugar. Make a well in the middle and pour in the milk, add the banana and orange rind and mix to a soft dough. The dough will be quite wet.

3 Turn out the dough onto a lightly floured work surface and, adding a little more flour if needed, roll out to 2 cm/¾ inch thick. Using a 6 cm/2½ inch biscuit cutter, cut out 12 scones, re-rolling the trimmings where possible, and place them on the prepared baking sheet. Brush with milk and bake in the preheated oven for 10–12 minutes.

4 Remove from the oven and leave to cool slightly, then halve the scones and fill with the raspberries.

Cherry & Sultana Scones

Makes 8

- 225 g/8 oz self-raising flour, plus extra for dusting
- 1 tbsp caster sugar
- pinch of salt
- 85 g/3 oz butter, cut into small pieces, plus extra for greasing
- 3 tbsp glacé cherries, chopped
- 3 tbsp sultanas
- 1 egg, lightly beaten
- 3 tbsp milk

1 Preheat the oven to 220°C/425°F/Gas Mark 7. Grease a baking sheet and line with baking paper.

2 Sift the flour, sugar and salt into a mixing bowl and rub in the butter with your fingertips until the mixture resembles breadcrumbs.

3 Stir in the glacé cherries and sultanas. Add the egg. Reserve 1 tablespoon of the milk for glazing, then add the remainder to the mixture. Mix well together to form a soft dough.

4 On a lightly floured work surface, roll out the dough to a thickness of 2 cm/¾ inch and cut out 8 circles using a 5-cm/2-inch round cutter.

5 Place the scones on the prepared baking sheet and brush the tops with the reserved milk.

6 Bake in the preheated oven for 8–10 minutes, or until the scones are golden brown. Transfer the scones to a wire rack to cool completely.

Tea Cakes

Makes 10–12

- 300 ml/½ pint milk
- 4 tsp dried yeast
- 55 g/2 oz caster sugar
- 450 g/1 lb strong plain flour
- 1 tsp salt
- 1 tsp ground mixed spice
- 115 g/4 oz currants
- 25 g/1 oz mixed peel, chopped
- 55 g/2 oz butter, melted
- 1 egg, beaten
- sugar glaze made from 2 tbsp sugar and 2 tbsp warm milk

1 Warm the milk in a saucepan until just tepid and add the yeast with 1 teaspoon of the sugar. Mix well and allow to froth in a warm place for 15 minutes.

2 Sift the flour, salt and spice into a large mixing bowl and add the currants, peel and the remaining sugar. Make a well in the centre of the dry ingredients and pour in the milk mixture, the melted butter and egg. Mix well using a wooden spoon at first and then by hand. Turn out onto a lightly floured surface and knead lightly until the dough is smooth and elastic.

3 Put the dough back into the bowl, cover with cling film and leave to rise in a warm place for 40–45 minutes until it has doubled in size. Knead the dough again lightly and divide into 10–12 even-sized buns, shaping well.

4 Preheat the oven to 220°C/425°F/ Gas Mark 7. Place the buns on two greased baking trays, cover with a damp tea towel or large plastic bags and allow to rise again for 30–40 minutes. Bake the tea cakes in the oven for 18–20 minutes until they are golden brown. Remove from the oven, place on a wire rack and glaze with the sugar glaze while still hot.

Eccles Cakes

Makes 10–12

- 400 g/14 oz ready-made puff pastry
- 2 tbsp plain flour, for dusting
- 55 g/2 oz butter, softened, plus extra for greasing
- 55 g/2 oz soft brown sugar
- 85 g/3 oz currants
- 25 g/1 oz mixed peel, chopped
- ½ tsp ground mixed spice (optional)
- 1 egg white, lightly beaten
- 1–2 tsp caster sugar

1 Preheat the oven to 220°C/425°F/ Gas Mark 7.

2 Roll out the pastry thinly, using the flour to dust the work surface and the rolling pin. Cut into rounds using a 9-cm/3½-inch cutter. Fold the trimmings carefully, re-roll and cut again to give a total of 10–12 rounds.

3 In a basin, mix together the butter and soft brown sugar until creamy, then add the dried fruit and mixed spice, if using.

4 Put a teaspoon of the filling in the centre of each pastry round. Draw the edges of the circles together and pinch the edges over the filling. Reshape each cake into a round.

5 Turn the cakes over and lightly roll them with the rolling pin until the currants just show through. Score several slits into each cake with a knife. Place the cakes on a greased baking tray and allow to rest for 10–15 minutes.

6 Brush the cakes with the egg white, sprinkle with 1 teaspoon of the caster sugar and bake at the top of the oven for about 15 minutes until golden brown and crisp.

7 Transfer to a wire rack and sprinkle with a little more sugar, if desired. Delicious straight from the oven, they also keep well in an airtight tin for a week and can be reheated before serving.

Brioche

Serves 6

brioche

- 225 g/8 oz strong white bread flour, plus extra for dusting
- ½ tsp salt
- 1 tbsp caster sugar
- 1½ tsp easy-blend dried yeast
- 2 eggs
- 2 tbsp lukewarm milk
- 55 g/2 oz unsalted butter, softened, plus extra for greasing

glaze

- 1 egg yolk
- 1 tbsp milk

1 Sift the flour and salt into a food processor and add the sugar and yeast. Lightly beat the eggs with the milk in a bowl. With the machine running, gradually add the egg and milk mixture and process, scraping down the sides as necessary, for 2–3 minutes, until a dough forms. Cut the butter into small pieces and add to the dough. Pulse the machine until the butter is fully incorporated.

2 Grease a bowl with butter. Shape the dough into a ball, put it in the bowl and put the bowl into a plastic bag or cover with a damp tea towel. Leave to rise in a warm place for 1 hour, until the dough has doubled in volume.

3 Grease a brioche tin with butter. Turn out the dough on to a lightly floured surface and knock back gently with your fist. Cut off about one-quarter of the dough and wrap in cling film. Knead the larger piece of dough, shape into a ball, place in the prepared tin and indent the top. Unwrap the smaller piece of dough, knead lightly into a pear shape and place on top of the indent to make the tête.

4 Put the tin into a plastic bag or cover with a damp tea towel and leave to rise in a warm place for 1 hour.

5 Preheat the oven to 220°C/425°F/Gas Mark 7. To make the glaze, beat the egg yolk with the milk, then brush over the top of the brioche. Bake for 40–45 minutes, until golden brown. Turn out on to a wire rack to cool.

Strawberry Jam

Serves 6

makes about 450 g/1 lb

- 1.5 kg/3 lb 5 oz ripe, unblemished whole strawberries, hulled and rinsed
- 2 freshly squeezed lemons, juice sieved
- 1.5 kg/3 lb 5 oz jam sugar
- 1 tsp butter

1 Place the strawberries in a preserving pan with the lemon juice, then simmer over a gentle heat for 15–20 minutes, stirring occasionally, until the fruit has collapsed and is very soft.

2 Add the sugar and heat, stirring occasionally, until the sugar has completely dissolved. Add the butter, then bring to the boil and boil rapidly for 10–20 minutes, or until the setting point is reached.

3 Test the mixture with a sugar thermometer – it should read 105ºC/221ºF for a good setting point. Alternatively, drop a teaspoonful of the mixture onto a cold saucer, place it in the refrigerator to cool, and then push it with your finger. If it forms a wrinkled skin, it is ready. If not, boil for a further minute and repeat.

4 Leave to cool for 8–10 minutes, skim then pot into warmed sterilized jars and cover the tops with waxed discs. When completely cold, cover with cellophane or lids, label and store in a cool place.

Orange Marmalade

Serves 6

makes about 4.5 kg/10 lb

- 1.5 kg/3 lb 5 oz Seville oranges, scrubbed
- juice of 2 large lemons
- 3.4 litres/6 pints water
- 2.7 kg/6 lb preserving sugar

1 Cut the oranges in half and squeeze out all the juice. Scoop out the pips from the orange peel shells and tie up in a small piece of muslin. Slice the peel into small strips and place in a preserving pan with the orange and lemon juice and water. Add the bag of pips.

2 Simmer gently for 1½ hours, or until the peel is very soft and the liquid has reduced by half. Remove the bag of pips, carefully squeezing to remove any juice. Add the sugar and heat, stirring, until the sugar has completely dissolved. Bring to the boil and boil rapidly for about 15 minutes, or until the setting point is reached.

3 Test the mixture with a sugar thermometer – it should read 105ºC/221ºF for a good setting point. Alternatively, drop a teaspoonful of the mixture onto a cold saucer, place it in the refrigerator to cool, and then push it with your finger. If it forms a wrinkled skin, it is ready. If not, boil for a further minute and repeat.

4 Leave to cool slightly, then pot into warmed sterilized jars and cover the tops with waxed discs. When completely cold, cover with cellophane or lids, label and store in a cool place.

Little & Large Cakes

Victoria Sponge Cake

Serves 8

- 175 g/6 oz self-raising flour
- 1 tsp baking powder
- 175 g/6 oz butter, softened, plus extra for greasing
- 175 g/6 oz golden caster sugar
- 3 eggs
- icing sugar, for dusting

filling

- 3 tbsp raspberry jam
- 300 ml/10 fl oz double cream, whipped
- 16 fresh strawberries, halved

1 Preheat the oven to 180°C/350°F/Gas Mark 4. Grease and line the bases of two 20-cm/8-inch sandwich tins.

2 Sift the flour and baking powder into a bowl and add the butter, sugar and eggs. Mix together, then beat well until smooth.

3 Divide the mixture evenly between the prepared tins and smooth the surfaces. Bake in the preheated oven for 25–30 minutes, or until well risen and golden brown, and the cakes feel springy when lightly pressed.

4 Leave to cool in the tins for 5 minutes, then turn out and peel off the lining paper. Transfer to wire racks to cool completely. Sandwich the cakes together with the raspberry jam, whipped double cream and strawberry halves. Dust with icing sugar and serve.

OVERNIGHT
STORE FRUITS.

COOKED.
STORE 2 MONTHS

Rich Fruit Cake

Serves 16

- 350 g/12 oz sultanas
- 225 g/8 oz raisins
- 115 g/4 oz ready-to-eat dried apricots, chopped
- 85 g/3 oz stoned dates, chopped
- 4 tbsp dark rum or brandy, plus extra for flavouring (optional)
- finely grated rind and juice of 1 orange
- 225 g/8 oz unsalted butter, plus extra for greasing
- 225 g/8 oz light muscovado sugar
- 4 eggs
- 70 g/2½ oz chopped mixed peel
- 85 g/3 oz glacé cherries, quartered
- 25 g/1 oz chopped glacé ginger or stem ginger
- 40 g/1½ oz blanched almonds, chopped
- 200 g/7 oz plain flour
- 1 tsp ground mixed spice

1 Place the sultanas, raisins, apricots and dates in a large bowl and stir in the rum, orange rind and orange juice. Cover and leave to soak for several hours or overnight.

2 Preheat the oven to 150°C/300°F/ Gas Mark 2. Grease and line a 20-cm/8-inch round deep cake tin.

3 Cream together the butter and sugar until light and fluffy. Gradually beat in the eggs, beating hard after each addition. Stir in the soaked fruits, mixed peel, glacé cherries, glacé ginger and blanched almonds.

4 Sift together the flour and mixed spice, then fold lightly and evenly into the mixture. Spoon the mixture into the prepared cake tin and level the surface, making a slight depression in the centre with the back of the spoon.

5 Bake in the preheated oven for 2¼–2¾ hours, or until the cake is beginning to shrink away from the sides and a skewer inserted into the centre comes out clean. Cool completely in the tin.

6 Turn out the cake and remove the lining paper. Wrap in greaseproof paper and foil, and store for at least two months before use. To add a richer flavour, prick the cake with a skewer and spoon over a couple of extra tablespoons of rum or brandy, if using, before storing.

Coffee & Walnut Cake

Serves 8

- 175 g/6 oz unsalted butter, plus extra for greasing
- 175 g/6 oz light muscovado sugar
- 3 large eggs, beaten
- 3 tbsp strong black coffee
- 175 g/6 oz self-raising flour
- 1½ tsp baking powder
- 115 g/4 oz walnut pieces
- walnut halves, to decorate

frosting

- 115 g/4 oz unsalted butter
- 200 g/7 oz icing sugar
- 1 tbsp strong black coffee
- ½ tsp vanilla extract

1 Preheat the oven to 180°C/350°F/Gas Mark 4. Grease and line the bases of two 20-cm/8-inch sandwich tins.

2 Cream together the butter and muscovado sugar until pale and fluffy. Gradually add the eggs, beating well after each addition. Beat in the coffee.

3 Sift the flour and baking powder into the mixture, then fold in lightly and evenly with a metal spoon. Fold in the walnut pieces.

4 Divide the mixture between the prepared cake tins and smooth level. Bake in the preheated oven for 20–25 minutes, or until golden brown and springy to the touch. Turn out onto a wire rack to cool.

5 For the frosting, beat together the butter, icing sugar, coffee and vanilla extract, mixing until smooth and creamy.

6 Use about half the mixture to sandwich the cakes together, then spread the remaining frosting on top and swirl with a palette knife. Decorate with walnut halves.

Frosted Carrot Cake

Serves 16

- 175 ml/6 fl oz sunflower oil, plus extra for greasing
- 175 g/6 oz light muscovado sugar
- 3 eggs, beaten
- 175 g/6 oz grated carrots
- 85 g/3 oz sultanas
- 55 g/2 oz walnut pieces
- grated rind of 1 orange
- 175 g/6 oz self-raising flour
- 1 tsp bicarbonate of soda
- 1 tsp ground cinnamon
- ½ tsp grated nutmeg
- strips of orange zest, to decorate

frosting

- 200 g/7 oz full-fat soft cheese
- 100 g/3½ oz icing sugar
- 2 tsp orange juice

1 Preheat the oven to 180°C/350°F/Gas Mark 4. Grease and line the base of a 23-cm/9-inch square cake tin.

2 In a large bowl beat together the oil, muscovado sugar and eggs. Stir in the grated carrots, sultanas, walnuts and orange rind.

3 Sift together the flour, bicarbonate of soda, cinnamon and nutmeg, then stir evenly into the carrot mixture.

4 Spoon the mixture into the prepared cake tin and bake in the preheated oven for 40–45 minutes, until well risen and firm to the touch.

5 Remove the cake from the oven and set on a wire rack for 5 minutes. Turn out onto the wire rack to cool completely.

6 For the frosting, combine the soft cheese, icing sugar and orange juice in a bowl and beat until smooth. Spread over the top of the cake and swirl with a palette knife. Decorate with strips of orange zest and serve cut into squares.

Lemon Drizzle Cake

Serves 12

- 2 eggs
- 175 g/6 oz caster sugar
- 150 g/5½ oz soft margarine, plus extra for greasing
- finely grated rind of 1 lemon
- 175 g/6 oz self-raising flour
- 125 ml/4 fl oz milk
- icing sugar, for dusting

syrup

- 140 g/5 oz icing sugar
- 50 ml/2 fl oz fresh lemon juice

1 Preheat the oven to 180°C/350°F/Gas Mark 4. Grease an 18-cm/7-inch square cake tin and line with non-stick baking paper.

2 Place the eggs, caster sugar and margarine in a mixing bowl and beat hard until smooth and fluffy. Stir in the lemon rind, then fold in the flour lightly and evenly. Stir in the milk, mixing evenly, then spoon into the prepared cake tin, smoothing level.

3 Bake in the preheated oven for 45–50 minutes, or until golden brown and firm to the touch. Remove from the oven and stand the tin on a wire rack.

4 To make the syrup, place the icing sugar and lemon juice in a small saucepan and heat gently, stirring until the sugar dissolves. Do not boil.

5 Prick the warm cake all over with a skewer, and spoon the hot syrup evenly over the top, allowing it to be absorbed.

6 Leave to cool completely in the tin, then turn out the cake, cut into 12 pieces and dust with a little icing sugar before serving.

Madeira Cake

Serves 8–10

- 175 g/6 oz unsalted butter, plus extra for greasing
- 175 g/6 oz caster sugar
- finely grated rind of 1 lemon
- 3 large eggs, beaten
- 115 g/4 oz plain flour
- 115 g/4 oz self-raising flour
- 2–3 tbsp brandy or milk
- 2 slices of citron peel

1 Preheat the oven to 160°C/325°F/Gas Mark 3. Grease and line an 18-cm/7-inch round deep cake tin.

2 Cream together the butter and sugar until pale and fluffy. Add the lemon rind and gradually beat in the eggs. Sift in the flours and fold in evenly, adding enough brandy to make a soft dropping consistency.

3 Spoon the mixture into the prepared tin and smooth the surface. Lay the slices of citron peel on top of the cake.

4 Bake in the preheated oven for 1–1¼ hours, or until well risen, golden brown and springy to the touch.

5 Cool in the tin for 10 minutes, then turn out and cool completely on a wire rack.

Vanilla Frosted Cupcakes

Makes 12

- 115 g/4 oz unsalted butter, softened
- 115 g/4 oz golden caster sugar
- 2 eggs, lightly beaten
- 115 g/4 oz self-raising flour
- 1 tbsp milk
- crystallized rose petals, to decorate

frosting

- 175 g/6 oz unsalted butter, softened
- 2 tsp vanilla extract
- 2 tbsp milk
- 300 g/10½ oz icing sugar, sifted

1 Preheat the oven to 180ºC/350ºF/Gas Mark 4. Line a 12-hole muffin tin with paper cases.

2 Place the butter and sugar in a bowl and beat together until light and fluffy. Gradually beat in the eggs. Sift in the flour and fold in gently using a metal spoon. Fold in the milk.

3 Spoon the mixture into the paper cases. Bake in the preheated oven for 15–20 minutes until golden brown and firm to the touch. Transfer to a cooling rack and leave to cool.

4 To make the frosting, put the butter, vanilla extract and milk in a large bowl. Using an electric hand whisk beat the mixture until smooth. Gradually beat in the icing sugar and continue beating for 2–3 minutes until the frosting is very light and creamy.

5 Spoon the frosting into a large piping bag fitted with a large star nozzle and pipe swirls of the frosting onto the top of each cupcake. Decorate each cupcake with crystallized rose petals.

Gingerbread Cupcakes

Makes 16

- 115 g/4 oz plain flour
- 2 tsp ground ginger
- ¾ tsp ground cinnamon
- 1 piece of stem ginger, finely chopped
- ¾ tsp bicarbonate of soda
- 4 tbsp milk
- 85 g/3 oz butter, softened
- 70 g/2½ oz soft dark brown sugar
- 2 tbsp black treacle
- 2 eggs, lightly beaten
- 1 piece of stem ginger, to decorate

icing

- 85 g/3 oz butter, softened
- 175 g/6 oz icing sugar
- 2 tbsp ginger syrup from the stem ginger jar

1 Preheat the oven to 160°C/325°F/Gas Mark 3. Put 16 paper baking cases in 2 bun trays, or place 16 double-layer paper cases on a baking tray.

2 Sift the flour, ground ginger and cinnamon together into a bowl. Add the chopped ginger and toss in the flour mixture until well coated. In a separate bowl, dissolve the bicarbonate of soda in the milk.

3 Put the butter and sugar in a bowl and beat together until fluffy. Beat in the treacle, then gradually add the eggs, beating well after each addition. Beat in the flour mixture, then gradually beat in the milk. Spoon the mixture into the paper cases.

4 Bake the cupcakes in the preheated oven for 20 minutes, or until well risen and golden brown. Transfer to a wire rack and leave to cool.

5 To make the icing, put the butter in a bowl and beat until fluffy. Sift in the icing sugar, add the ginger syrup and beat together until smooth and creamy. Slice the stem ginger into thin slivers or chop finely.

6 When the cupcakes are cold, spread the icing on top of each cupcake, then decorate with pieces of the ginger.

Pastries & Fancies

Vanilla Macaroons

Makes 16

- 75 g/2¾ oz ground almonds
- 115 g/4 oz icing sugar
- 2 large egg whites
- 50 g/1¾ oz caster sugar
- ½ tsp vanilla extract

filling

- 55 g/2 oz unsalted butter, softened
- ½ tsp vanilla extract
- 115 g/4 oz icing sugar, sifted

1 Place the ground almonds and icing sugar in a food processor and process for 15 seconds. Sift the mixture into a bowl. Line two baking sheets with baking paper.

2 Place the egg whites in a large bowl and whisk until holding soft peaks. Gradually whisk in the caster sugar to make a firm, glossy meringue. Whisk in the vanilla extract.

3 Using a spatula, fold the almond mixture into the meringue one third at a time. When all the dry ingredients are thoroughly incorporated, continue to cut and fold the mixture until it forms a shiny batter with a thick, ribbon-like consistency.

4 Pour the mixture into a piping bag fitted with a 1-cm/½-inch plain nozzle. Pipe 32 small rounds onto the prepared baking sheets. Tap the baking sheets firmly onto a work surface to remove air bubbles. Leave at room temperature for 30 minutes. Preheat the oven to 160°C/325°F/Gas Mark 3.

5 Bake in the preheated oven for 10–15 minutes. Cool for 10 minutes, then carefully peel the macaroons off the baking paper. Leave to cool completely.

6 To make the filling, beat the butter and vanilla extract in a bowl until pale and fluffy. Gradually beat in the icing sugar until smooth and creamy. Use to sandwich pairs of macaroons together.

Chocolate Hazelnut Macaroons

Makes 16

- 50 g/1¾ oz ground almonds
- 25 g/1 oz hazelnuts, finely ground, plus 1 tbsp chopped for decoration
- 115 g/4 oz icing sugar
- 2 large egg whites
- 50 g/1¾ oz caster sugar
- 6 tbsp hazelnut and chocolate spread

1 Place the ground almonds, ground hazelnuts and icing sugar in a food processor and process for 15 seconds. Sift the mixture into a bowl. Line two baking sheets with baking paper.

2 Place the egg whites in a large bowl and whisk until holding soft peaks. Gradually whisk in the caster sugar until you have a firm, glossy meringue.

3 Using a spatula, fold the almond mixture into the meringue one third at a time. When all the dry ingredients are thoroughly incorporated, continue to cut and fold the mixture until it forms a shiny batter with a thick, ribbon-like consistency.

4 Pour the mixture into a piping bag fitted with a 1-cm/½-inch plain nozzle. Pipe 32 small rounds onto the prepared baking sheets. Tap the baking sheets firmly onto a work surface to remove air bubbles. Sprinkle over the chopped hazelnuts. Leave at room temperature for 30 minutes. Preheat the oven to 160°C/325°F/Gas Mark 3.

5 Bake in the preheated oven for 10–15 minutes. Cool for 10 minutes, then carefully peel the macaroons off the baking paper. Leave to cool completely.

6 Sandwich pairs of macaroons together with the hazelnut and chocolate spread and serve immediately.

Mini Florentines

Makes 40

- 6 tbsp butter, plus extra for greasing
- plain flour, for dusting
- 75 g/2¾ oz caster sugar
- 2 tbsp sultanas or raisins
- 2 tbsp chopped glacé cherries
- 2 tbsp chopped stem ginger
- 25 g/1 oz sunflower seeds
- 100 g/3½ oz flaked almonds
- 2 tbsp double cream
- 175 g/6 oz plain or milk chocolate, broken into pieces

1 Preheat the oven to 180°C/350°F/Gas Mark 4. Grease and flour 2 baking trays or line with greaseproof paper.

2 Place the butter in a small saucepan and heat gently until melted. Add the sugar, stir until dissolved, then bring the mixture to the boil. Remove from the heat and stir in the sultanas, cherries, ginger, sunflower seeds and almonds. Mix well, then beat in the cream.

3 Place small teaspoons of the fruit and nut mixture on to the prepared baking trays, allowing plenty of room for the mixture to spread during baking. Bake in the preheated oven for 10–12 minutes, or until light golden in colour.

4 Remove from the oven and, while still hot, use a circular biscuit cutter to pull in the edges to form perfect circles. Leave to cool and go crisp before removing from the baking trays.

5 Put the chocolate in a heatproof bowl set over a saucepan of gently simmering water and stir until melted. Spread most of the chocolate on to a sheet of greaseproof paper. When the chocolate is on the point of setting, place the biscuits flat-side down on the chocolate and let it harden completely.

6 Cut around the florentines and remove from the greaseproof paper. Spread a little more chocolate on the coated side of the florentines and use a fork to mark waves in the chocolate. Leave to set. Keep cool.

Madeleines

Makes about 30

- 3 eggs
- 1 egg yolk
- 1 tsp vanilla extract
- 140 g/5 oz caster sugar
- 140 g/5 oz plain flour
- 1 tsp baking powder
- 140 g/5 oz unsalted butter, melted and cooled, plus extra for greasing

1 Preheat the oven to 190°C/375°F/Gas Mark 5. Lightly grease 30 holes in two to three standard-sized madeleine tins.

2 Place the eggs, egg yolk, vanilla extract and sugar in a large bowl and whisk with an electric hand mixer until very pale and thick.

3 Sift in the flour and baking powder and fold in lightly and evenly using a metal spoon. Fold in the melted butter evenly.

4 Spoon the mixture into the prepared tins, filling to about three-quarters full. Bake in the preheated oven for 8–10 minutes, until risen and golden.

5 Remove the cakes carefully from the tins and cool on a wire rack. They are best served the day they are made.

Pistachio & Almond Tuiles

Makes 12

- 1 egg white
- 55 g/2 oz golden caster sugar
- 25 g/1 oz plain flour
- 25 g/1 oz pistachio nuts, finely chopped
- 25 g/1 oz ground almonds
- ½ tsp almond extract
- 40 g/1½ oz unsalted butter, melted and cooled

1 Preheat the oven to 160°C/325°F/Gas Mark 3. Line two baking trays with baking paper.

2 Whisk the egg white lightly with the sugar, then stir in the flour, pistachios, ground almonds, almond extract and butter, mixing to a soft paste.

3 Place walnut-sized spoonfuls of the mixture on the prepared baking trays and use the back of the spoon to spread as thinly as possible. Bake in the preheated oven for 10–15 minutes, until pale golden.

4 Quickly lift each biscuit with a palette knife and place over the side of a rolling pin to shape into a curve. When set, transfer to a wire rack to cool.

Cream Palmiers

Makes 8

- 40 g/1½ oz granulated sugar
- 225 g/8 oz ready-made puff pastry
- 400 ml/14 fl oz whipping cream or double cream
- 1 tbsp icing sugar, sifted
- few drops vanilla extract
- 2 tbsp strawberry jam

1 Preheat the oven to 220°C/425°F/Gas Mark 7. Dust the work surface with half the sugar and roll the pastry out on the sugared work surface to a 25 x 30-cm/ 10 x 12-inch rectangle.

2 Sprinkle the rest of the sugar over the pastry and roll gently over it with the rolling pin. Roll the two short sides of the pastry into the centre until they meet, moisten the edges that meet with a little water and press together gently. Cut across the roll into 16 even-sized slices.

3 Place the slices, cut side down, on a dampened baking tray. Use a rolling pin to flatten each one slightly.

4 Bake in the preheated oven for 15–18 minutes until crisp and golden brown, turning the palmiers over halfway through cooking so that both sides caramelize. Transfer to a wire rack to cool.

5 Whip the cream, icing sugar and vanilla extract together until softly peaking. Sandwich the palmiers together with the jam and whipped cream and serve within 2–3 hours of filling.

Chocolate Éclairs

Makes 12

choux pastry

- 150 ml/5 fl oz water
- 70 g/2½ oz butter, cut into small pieces, plus extra for greasing
- 100 g/3½ oz plain flour, sifted
- 2 eggs

pastry cream

- 2 eggs, lightly beaten
- 4 tbsp caster sugar
- 2 tbsp cornflour
- 300 ml/10 fl oz milk
- ¼ tsp vanilla extract

icing

- 2 tbsp butter
- 1 tbsp milk
- 1 tbsp cocoa powder
- 55 g/2 oz icing sugar
- 50 g/1¾ oz white chocolate, broken into pieces

1 Preheat the oven to 200°C/400°F/Gas Mark 6. Lightly grease a baking sheet.

2 Place the water in a saucepan, add the butter and heat gently until the butter melts. Bring to a rolling boil, then remove the saucepan from the heat and add the flour all at once, beating well until the mixture leaves the sides of the saucepan and forms a ball. Leave to cool slightly, then gradually beat in the eggs to form a smooth, glossy mixture. Spoon into a large piping bag fitted with a 1-cm/½-inch plain nozzle.

3 Sprinkle the baking sheet with a little water. Pipe 12 éclairs 7.5 cm/3 inches long, spaced well apart. Bake for 30–35 minutes, or until crisp and golden. Make a small slit in the side of each éclair to let the steam escape. Leave to cool on a wire rack.

4 Meanwhile, make the pastry cream. Whisk the eggs and sugar until thick and creamy, then fold in the cornflour. Heat the milk until almost boiling and pour onto the eggs, whisking. Transfer to the saucepan and cook over a low heat, stirring until thick. Remove the saucepan from the heat and stir in the vanilla extract. Cover with baking paper and leave to cool.

5 To make the icing, melt the butter with the milk in a saucepan. Remove from the heat and stir in the cocoa and sugar. Split the éclairs lengthways and pipe in the pastry cream. Spread the icing over the top of the éclairs. Melt a little white chocolate in a heatproof bowl set over a saucepan of gently simmering water, then drizzle over the chocolate icing and leave to set. Serve immediately.

Summer Fruit Tartlets

Makes 12

pastry

- 200 g/7 oz plain flour, plus extra for dusting
- 85 g/3 oz icing sugar
- 55 g/2 oz ground almonds
- 115 g/4 oz butter
- 1 egg yolk
- 1 tbsp milk

filling

- 225 g/8 oz cream cheese
- icing sugar, to taste, plus extra for dusting
- 350 g/12 oz fresh summer fruits, such as red and whitecurrants, blueberries, raspberries and small strawberries

1 To make the pastry, sift the flour and icing sugar into a bowl. Stir in the ground almonds. Add the butter and rub in until the mixture resembles breadcrumbs. Add the egg yolk and milk and work in with a palette knife, then mix with your fingertips until the dough binds together. Wrap the dough in clingfilm and leave to chill in the refrigerator for 30 minutes.

2 Preheat the oven to 200°C/400°F/Gas Mark 6. Roll out the pastry on a lightly floured work surface and use it to line 12 deep tartlet or individual brioche tins. Prick the bases with a fork. Press a piece of foil into each tartlet, covering the edges.

3 Bake in the preheated oven for 10–15 minutes, or until light golden brown. Remove the foil and bake for a further 2–3 minutes. Transfer the pastry cases to a wire rack to cool.

4 To make the filling, place the cream cheese and icing sugar in a bowl and mix together. Place a spoonful of filling in each pastry case and arrange the fruit on top. Dust the tartlets with sifted icing sugar and serve immediately.